let's cook

pasta

Tom
Bridge

p

Contents

Spaghetti alla Carbonara

*Ensure that all of the cooked ingredients are as hot as possible
before adding the eggs, so that they cook on contact.*

Serves 4

INGREDIENTS

425 g/15 oz dried spaghetti
2 tbsp olive oil
1 large onion, thinly sliced
2 garlic cloves, chopped
175 g/6 oz rindless bacon, cut into
  thin strips

25 g/1 oz/2 tbsp butter
175 g/6 oz mushrooms, thinly sliced
300 ml/$\frac{1}{2}$ pint/1$\frac{1}{4}$ cups double
  (heavy) cream
3 eggs, beaten

100 g /3$\frac{1}{2}$ oz/1 cup freshly grated
  Parmesan cheese, plus extra to
  serve (optional)
salt and pepper
fresh sage sprigs, to garnish

1 Warm a large serving dish or bowl. Bring a large pan of lightly salted water to the boil. Add the spaghetti and 1 tbsp of the oil and cook until tender, but still firm to the bite. Drain, return to the pan and keep warm.

2 Meanwhile, heat the remaining oil in a frying pan (skillet) over a medium heat. Add the onion and fry until it is transparent. Add the garlic and bacon and fry until the bacon is crisp. Transfer to the warm plate.

3 Melt the butter in the frying pan (skillet). Add the mushrooms and fry, stirring occasionally, for 3-4 minutes. Return the bacon mixture to the pan. Cover and keep warm.

4 Mix together the cream, eggs and cheese in a large bowl and then season to taste with salt and pepper.

5 Working very quickly, tip the spaghetti into the bacon and mushroom mixture and pour over the eggs. Toss the spaghetti quickly into the egg and cream mixture, using 2 forks, and serve immediately. If you wish, serve with extra grated Parmesan cheese.

COOK'S TIP

The key to success with this recipe is not to overcook the egg. That is why it is important to keep all the ingredients hot enough just to cook the egg and to work rapidly to avoid scrambling it.

Smoked Ham Linguini

Served with freshly made Italian bread or tossed with pesto, this makes a mouth-watering light lunch.

Serves 4

INGREDIENTS

450 g/1 lb dried linguini
450 g/1 lb green broccoli
  florets (flowerets)

225g/8 oz Italian smoked ham
150 ml/^{1}/$_4$ pint/^{5}/$_8$ cup Italian Cheese
  Sauce (see Cook's Tip, below right)

salt and pepper
Italian bread, to serve

1 Bring a large pan of lightly salted water to the boil. Add the linguini and broccoli florets and cook for 10 minutes, until the linguini is tender, but still firm to the bite.

2 Drain the linguini and broccoli thoroughly, set aside and keep warm.

3 Meanwhile, make the Italian Cheese Sauce (see Cook's Tip, right).

4 Cut the Italian smoked ham into thin strips. Toss the linguini, broccoli and ham into the Italian Cheese Sauce and gently warm through over a very low heat.

5 Transfer the pasta mixture to a warm serving dish. Sprinkle with black pepper and serve with Italian bread.

COOK'S TIP

There are many types of Italian bread which woukd be suitable to serve with this dish. Ciabatta is made with olive oil and is available plain and with different ingredients, such as olives or sun-dried tomatoes.

COOK'S TIP

For Italian Cheese Sauce, melt 2 tbsp butter in a pan and stir in 25 g/1/ oz/¼ cup plain (all purpose) flour. Cook, stirring, over a low heat until the roux is light in colour and crumbly in texture. Stir in 300 ml/½ pint/1¼ cups hot milk. Cook, stirring, for 15 minutes until thick and smooth. Add a pinch of nutmeg, a pinch of dried thyme, 2 tbsp white wine vinegar and season. Stir in 3 tbsp double (heavy) cream and mix. Stir in 60 g/2 oz/½ cup grated Mozzarella cheese, 60 g/2 oz/⅔ cup grated Parmesan cheese, 1 tsp English mustard and 2 tbsp soured cream.

Orecchiette with Bacon & Tomatoes

*As this dish cooks, the mouth-watering aroma of
bacon, sweet tomatoes and oregano is a feast in itself.*

Serves 4

INGREDIENTS

900 g/2 lb small, sweet tomatoes
6 slices rindless smoked bacon
60 g/2 oz/4 tbsp butter
1 onion, chopped

1 garlic clove, crushed
4 fresh oregano sprigs,
  finely chopped
450 g/1 lb/4 cups dried orecchiette

1 tbsp olive oil
salt and pepper
freshly grated Pecorino cheese,
  to serve

1 Blanch the tomatoes in boiling water. Drain, skin and seed the tomatoes, then roughly chop the flesh. Chop the bacon into small dice.

2 Melt the butter in a saucepan. Add the bacon and fry until it is golden. Add the onion and garlic and fry over a medium heat for 5-7 minutes, until softened.

3 Add the tomatoes and oregano to the pan and then season to taste with salt and pepper. Lower the heat and simmer for 10-12 minutes.

4 Bring a large pan of lightly salted water to the boil. Add the orecchiette and oil and cook for 12 minutes, until just tender, but still firm to the bite. Drain the pasta and transfer to a warm serving dish or bowl. Spoon over the bacon and tomato sauce, toss to coat and serve with the cheese.

VARIATION

You could also use 450 g/1 lb spicy Italian sausages. Squeeze the meat out of the skins and add to the pan in step 2 instead of the bacon.

COOK'S TIP

For an authentic Italian flavour use pancetta, rather than ordinary bacon. This kind of bacon is streaked with fat and adds rich undertones of flavour to many traditional dishes. It is available both smoked and unsmoked and can be bought in a single, large piece or cut into slices. You can buy it in some supermarkets and all Italian delicatessens.

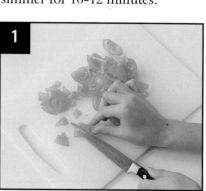

Spinach & Ricotta Shells

This is a classic combination in which the smooth, creamy cheese balances the sharper taste of the spinach.

Serves 4

INGREDIENTS

400 g/14 oz dried lumache
   rigate grande
5 tbsp olive oil
60/g 2 oz/1 cup fresh
   white breadcrumbs

125 ml/4 fl oz/^{1}/$_2$ cup milk
300 g/10^1/$_2$ oz frozen spinach,
   thawed and drained
225 g/8 oz/1 cup ricotta cheese
pinch of freshly grated nutmeg

400 g/14 oz can chopped
   tomatoes, drained
1 garlic clove, crushed
salt and pepper

1 Bring a large saucepan of lightly salted water to the boil. Add the lumache and 1 tbsp of the olive oil and cook until just tender, but still firm to the bite. Drain the pasta, refresh under cold water and set aside.

2 Put the breadcrumbs, milk and 3 tbsp of the remaining olive oil in a food processor and work to combine.

3 Add the spinach and ricotta cheese to the food processor and work to a smooth mixture.

Transfer to a bowl, stir in the nutmeg, and season with salt and pepper to taste.

4 Mix together the tomatoes, garlic and remaining oil and spoon the mixture into the base of an ovenproof dish.

5 Using a teaspoon, fill the lumache with the spinach and ricotta mixture and arrange on top of the tomato mixture in the dish. Cover and bake in a preheated oven at 180°C/350°F/Gas 4 for 20 minutes. Serve hot.

COOK'S TIP

Ricotta is a creamy Italian cheese traditionally made from ewes' milk whey. It is soft and white, with a smooth texture and a slightly sweet flavour. It should be used with 2–3 days of purchase.

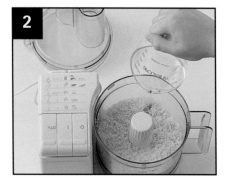

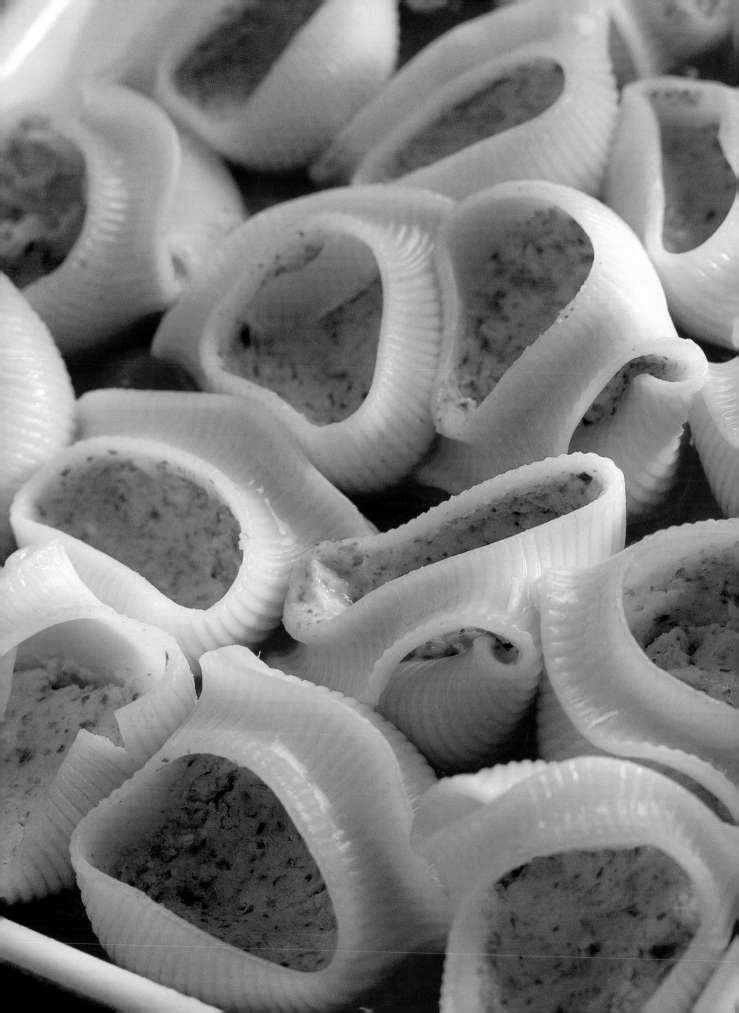

Tricolour Timballini

*An unusual way of serving pasta, these cheese moulds
are excellent with a crunchy salad for a light lunch.*

Serves 4

INGREDIENTS

15 g/$^{1}/_{2}$ oz/1 tbsp butter, softened
60 g/2 oz/1 cup dried white
   breadcrumbs
175 g/6 oz dried tricolour spaghetti,
   broken into 5 cm/2 inch lengths
3 tbsp olive oil
300 ml/$^{1}/_{2}$ pint/1$^{1}/_{4}$ cups Béchamel
   Sauce

1 egg yolk
125 g/4 oz/1 cup grated Gruyère
   (Swiss) cheese
1 onion, finely chopped
1 bay leaf
150 ml/$^{1}/_{4}$ pint/$^{5}/_{8}$ cup dry
   white wine

150 ml/$^{1}/_{4}$ pint/$^{5}/_{8}$ cup passata
   (sieved tomatoes)
1 tbsp tomato purée (paste)
salt and pepper
fresh flat leaf parsley sprigs,
   to garnish

1 Grease four 180 ml/6 fl oz/
$^{3}/_{4}$ cup moulds or ramekins
with the butter. Evenly coat the
insides with half the breadcrumbs.

2 Bring a saucepan of lightly
salted water to the boil. Add
the spaghetti and 1 tbsp of the oil
and cook until just tender. Drain
and transfer to a mixing bowl.

3 Add the egg yolk and cheese
to the pasta and season. Pour
the Béchamel sauce into the bowl
and mix. Spoon the mixture into
the ramekins and sprinkle over the
remaining breadcrumbs.

4 Stand the ramekins on a
baking (cookie) sheet and
bake in a preheated oven at 220°C/
425°F/Gas 7 for 20 minutes. Set
aside for 10 minutes.

5 Meanwhile, make the sauce.
Heat the remaining oil in a
pan and gently fry the onion and
bay leaf for 2-3 minutes.

6 Stir in the wine, passata
(sieved tomatoes) and tomato
purée (paste) and season. Simmer
for 20 minutes, until thickened.
Remove and discard the bay leaf.

7 Turn the timballini out on to
individual serving plates,
garnish with the parsley and serve
with the tomato sauce.

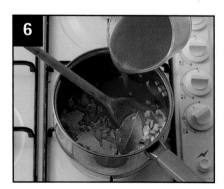

Tagliarini with Gorgonzola

This simple, creamy pasta sauce is a classic Italian recipe.

Serves 4

INGREDIENTS

25 g/1 oz/2 tbsp butter
225 g/8 oz Gorgonzola cheese,
   roughly crumbled
150 ml/¼ pint/⅝ cup double
   (heavy) cream

30 ml/2 tbsp dry white wine
1 tsp cornflour (cornstarch)
4 fresh sage sprigs, finely chopped
400 g/14 oz dried tagliarini
2 tbsp olive oil

salt and white pepper

1 Melt the butter in a heavy-based saucepan. Stir in 175 g/6 oz of the Gorgonzola cheese and melt, over a low heat, for about 2 minutes.

2 Add the cream, wine and cornflour (cornstarch) and beat with a whisk until fully incorporated.

3 Stir in the sage and season to taste with salt and white pepper. Bring to the boil over a low heat, whisking constantly, until the sauce thickens. Remove from the heat and set aside while you cook the pasta.

4 Bring a large saucepan of lightly salted water to the boil. Add the tagliarini and 1 tbsp of the olive oil. Cook the pasta for 12–14 minutes or until just tender, drain thoroughly and toss in the remaining olive oil. Transfer the pasta to a serving dish and keep warm.

5 Return the saucepan containing the sauce to a low heat to reheat the sauce, whisking constantly. Spoon the Gorgonzola sauce over the tagliarini, generously sprinkle over the remaining cheese and serve immediately.

COOK'S TIP

Gorgonzola is one of the world's oldest veined cheeses and, arguably, its finest. When buying, always check that it is creamy yellow with delicate green veining. Avoid hard or discoloured cheese. It should have a rich, piquant aroma, not a bitter smell. If you find Gorgonzola too strong or rich, you could substitute Danish blue.

Gnocchi Romana

This is a traditional recipe but, for a less rich version, omit the eggs.

Serves 4

INGREDIENTS

700 ml/1¼ pints/3⅛ cups milk
pinch of freshly grated nutmeg
90 g/3 oz/6 tbsp butter, plus extra
   for greasing

250 g/8 oz/1¼ cups semolina
125 g/4½ oz/1½ cups grated
   Parmesan cheese
2 eggs, beaten

60 g/2 oz/½ cup grated Gruyère
   (Swiss) cheese
salt and pepper
fresh basil sprigs, to garnish

1 Pour the milk into a saucepan and bring to the boil. Remove the pan from the heat and stir in the nutmeg, 25 g/1 oz/2 tbsp of the butter and salt and pepper to taste.

2 Gradually stir the semolina into the milk, whisking to prevent lumps forming, and return the pan to a low heat. Simmer, stirring constantly, for about 10 minutes, until very thick.

3 Beat 60 g/2 oz/⅔ cup of Parmesan cheese into the semolina mixture, then beat in the eggs. Continue beating the mixture until smooth. Set the mixture aside for a few minutes to cool slightly.

4 Spread out the semolina mixture in an even layer on a sheet of baking parchment or in a large, oiled baking tin (pan), smoothing the surface with a damp spatula – it should be about 1 cm/½ inch thick. Set aside to cool completely, then leave to chill in the refrigerator for 1 hour.

5 Once chilled, cut out rounds of gnocchi, measuring about 4 cm/1½ inches in diameter, using a plain, greased pastry cutter.

6 Grease a shallow ovenproof dish or 4 individual dishes. Lay the gnocchi trimmings in the base of the dish or dishes and cover with overlapping rounds of gnocchi.

7 Melt the remaining butter and drizzle over the gnocchi. Sprinkle over the remaining Parmesan cheese, then sprinkle over the Gruyère (Swiss) cheese.

8 Bake in a preheated oven at 200°C/400°F/Gas 6 for 25-30 minutes, until the top is crisp and golden brown. Serve hot, garnished with the basil.

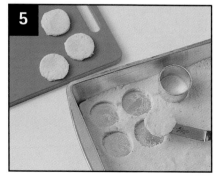

Baked Rigatoni Filled with Tuna & Ricotta Cheese

*Ribbed tubes of pasta are filled with fish and
cheese and then baked in a creamy sauce.*

Serves 4

INGREDIENTS

butter, for greasing
450 g/1 lb dried rigatoni
1 tbsp olive oil
200 g /7 oz can flaked tuna, drained

225 g/ 8 oz ricotta cheese
125 ml/4 fl oz/^{1}/$_2$ cup double
   (heavy) cream
225 g/8 oz/2^2/$_3$ cups grated
   Parmesan cheese

125 g/4 oz sun-dried tomatoes,
   drained sliced
salt and black pepper

1 Lightly grease an ovenproof
dish with butter.

2 Bring a large saucepan of
lightly salted water to the
boil. Add the rigatoni and olive oil
and cook until just tender, but still
firm to the bite. Drain the pasta
and set aside until cool enough
to handle.

3 In a bowl, mix together the
tuna and ricotta cheese to
form a soft paste. Spoon the

mixture into a piping bag and use
to fill the rigatoni. Arrange the
filled pasta tubes side by side in the
prepared ovenproof dish.

4 To make the sauce, mix the
cream and Parmesan cheese
and season. Spoon the sauce over
the rigatoni and top with the sun-
dried tomatoes arranged in a criss-
cross pattern. Bake in a preheated
oven at 200°C/400°F/Gas 6 for
20 minutes. Serve hot straight
from the dish.

VARIATION

*For a vegetarian alternative of this
recipe, simply substitute a mixture
of stoned (pitted) and chopped
black olives and chopped walnuts
for the tuna. Follow exactly the
same method cooking method.*

Spaghetti with Anchovy & Pesto Sauce

This is an ideal dish for cooks in a hurry and for those who do not have much time for shopping, as it is prepared in minutes from store-cupboard ingredients.

Serves 4

INGREDIENTS

90 ml/3 fl oz olive oil
2 garlic cloves, crushed
60 g/2 oz can anchovy fillets, drained
450 g/1 lb dried spaghetti
60 g/2 oz Pesto Sauce

2 tbsp finely chopped fresh oregano
90 g/3 oz/1 cup grated Parmesan
 cheese, plus extra for
 serving (optional)

salt and pepper
2 fresh oregano sprigs, to garnish

---

1 Reserve 1 tbsp of the oil and heat the remainder in a small saucepan. Add the garlic and fry for 3 minutes.

2 Lower the heat, stir in the anchovies and cook, stirring occasionally, until the anchovies have disintegrated.

3 Bring a large saucepan of lightly salted water to the boil. Add the spaghetti and the remaining olive oil and cook until just tender, but still firm to the bite.

4 Add the Pesto Sauce and chopped fresh oregano to the anchovy mixture and then season with black pepper to taste.

5 Drain the spaghetti, using a slotted spoon, and transfer to a warm serving dish. Pour the Pesto Sauce over the spaghetti and then sprinkle over the grated Parmesan cheese.

6 Garnish with oregano sprigs and serve with extra cheese, if using.

VARIATION

For a vegetarian alternative of this recipe, simply substitute drained sun-dried tomatoes for the anchovy fillets.

COOK'S TIP

If you find canned anchovies much too salty, soak them in a saucer of cold milk for 5 minutes, drain and pat dry with kitchen paper (kitchen towels) before using.

Spaghetti Bolognese

You can use this classic meat sauce for lasagne, cannelloni or any other baked pasta dishes.

Serves 4

INGREDIENTS

3 tbsp olive oil
2 garlic cloves, crushed
1 large onion, finely chopped
1 carrot, diced
225 g/8 oz/2 cups lean minced
 (ground) beef, veal or chicken

85 g/3 oz chicken livers,
 finely chopped
100 g/3^1/$_2$ oz lean, Parma ham
 (prosciutto), diced
150 ml/^{1}/$_4$ pint/^{5}/$_8$ cup Marsala

285 g/10 oz can chopped
 plum tomatoes
1 tbsp chopped fresh basil leaves
2 tbsp tomato purée (paste)
salt and pepper
450 g/1 lb dried spaghetti

1 Heat 2 tbsp of the olive oil in a large saucepan. Add the garlic, onion and carrot and fry for 6 minutes.

2 Add the minced (ground) beef, veal or chicken, chicken livers and Parma ham (prosciutto) to the pan and cook over a medium heat for 12 minutes, until well browned.

3 Stir in the Marsala, tomatoes, basil and tomato purée (paste) and cook for 4 minutes. Season to taste with salt and pepper. Cover and simmer for about 30 minutes.

4 Remove the lid from the pan, stir and simmer for a further 15 minutes.

5 Meanwhile, bring a large pan of lightly salted water to the boil. Add the spaghetti and the remaining oil and cook for about 12 minutes, until tender, but still firm to the bite. Drain and transfer to a serving dish. Pour the sauce over the pasta, toss and serve hot.

VARIATION

Chicken livers are an essential ingredient in a classic Bolognese sauce to which they add richness. However, if you prefer not to use them, you can substitute the same quantity of minced (ground) beef.

Creamed Strips of Sirloin with Rigatoni

*This quick and easy dish tastes superb and would
make a delicious treat for a special occasion.*

Serves 4

INGREDIENTS

75 g/3 oz/6 tbsp butter
450 g/1 lb sirloin steak, trimmed and
 cut into thin strips
175 g/6 oz button mushrooms, sliced
1 tsp mustard
pinch of freshly grated root ginger

2 tbsp dry sherry
150 ml/¼ pint/⅝ cup double
 (heavy) cream
salt and pepper
4 slices hot toast, cut into triangles,
 to serve

PASTA:
450 g/1 lb dried rigatoni
2 tbsp olive oil
2 fresh basil sprigs
115 g/4 oz/8 tbsp butter

1 Preheat the oven to
90°C/375°F/Gas 5. Melt the
butter in a large frying pan
(skillet) and gently fry the steak
over a low heat, stirring
frequently, for 6 minutes. Using a
slotted spoon, transfer the steak to
an ovenproof dish and keep warm.

2 Add the sliced mushrooms to
the frying pan (skillet) and
cook for 2–3 minutes in the juices
remaining in the pan. Add the
mustard, ginger, salt and pepper.
Cook for 2 minutes, then add the
sherry and cream. Cook for a
further 3 minutes, then pour the
cream sauce over the steak.

3 Bake the steak and cream
mixture for 10 minutes.

4 Meanwhile, cook the pasta.
Bring a large saucepan of
lightly salted water to the boil. Add
the rigatoni, olive oil and 1 of the
basil sprigs and boil rapidly for
10 minutes, until tender but still
firm to the bite. Drain the pasta
and transfer to a warm serving
dish. Toss the pasta with the butter
and garnish with the remaining
basil sprig.

5 Serve the steak with the
triangles of warm toast. Serve
the rigatoni separately.

COOK'S TIP

*Dried pasta will keep for up to 6
months. Keep it in the packet and
reseal it once you have opened it, or
transfer the pasta to an airtight jar.*

Fresh Spaghetti with Italian Meatballs in Tomato Sauce

This well-loved Italian dish is famous across the world. Make the most of it by using high-quality steak for the meatballs.

Serves 4

INGREDIENTS

150 g/5¹/₂ oz/2¹/₂ cups brown breadcrumbs
150 ml/¹/₄ pint/⁵/₈ cup milk
25 g/1 oz/2 tbsp butter
25 g/1 oz/¹/₄ cup wholemeal (whole-wheat) flour

200 ml/7 fl oz/⁷/₈ cup beef stock
400 g/14 oz can chopped tomatoes
2 tbsp tomato purée (paste)
1 tsp sugar
1 tbsp finely chopped fresh tarragon
1 large onion, chopped

450 g/1 lb/4 cups minced steak
1 tsp paprika
4 tbsp olive oil
450 g/1 lb fresh spaghetti
salt and pepper
fresh tarragon sprigs, to garnish

1 Place the breadcrumbs in a bowl, add the milk and set aside to soak for 30 minutes.

2 Melt half the butter in a pan. Add the flour and cook, stirring constantly, for 2 minutes. Gradually stir in the beef stock and cook, stirring constantly, for a further 5 minutes. Add the tomatoes, tomato purée (paste), sugar and tarragon. Season well and simmer for 25 minutes.

3 Mix the onion, steak and paprika into the breadcrumbs and season to taste. Shape the mixture into 14 meatballs.

4 Heat the oil and remaining butter in a frying pan (skillet) and fry the meatballs, turning frequently, until brown all over. Place them in a deep casserole, pour over the tomato sauce, cover and bake in a preheated oven at 180°C/350°F/Gas 4 for 25 minutes.

5 Bring a large saucepan of lightly salted water to the boil. Add the fresh spaghetti, bring back to the boil and cook for about 2–3 minutes, until tender, but still firm to the bite.

6 Meanwhile, remove the meatballs from the oven and allow them to cool for 3 minutes. Serve the meatballs and their sauce with the spaghetti, garnished with tarragon sprigs.

Sicilian Spaghetti

This delicious Sicilian dish originated as a handy way of using up leftover cooked pasta.

Serves 4

INGREDIENTS

150 ml/¼ pint/⅝ cup olive oil, plus
  extra for brushing
2 aubergines (eggplant)
350 g/12 oz/3 cups minced
  (ground) beef
1 onion, chopped
2 garlic cloves, crushed
2 tbsp tomato purée (paste)
400 g/14 oz can chopped tomatoes

1 tsp Worcestershire sauce
1 tsp chopped fresh marjoram or
  oregano or ½ tsp dried marjoram
  or oregano
60 g/2 oz/½ cup stoned (pitted)
  black olives, sliced
1 green, red or yellow (bell) pepper,
  cored, seeded and chopped
175 g/6 oz dried spaghetti

115 g/4 oz/1 cup freshly grated
  Parmesan cheese
salt and pepper
fresh oregano or parsley sprigs,
  to garnish

---

1 Brush a 20 cm/8 inch loose-based round cake tin (pan) with oil, line the base with baking parchment and brush with oil.

2 Slice the aubergines (eggplant). Heat a little oil in a pan and fry the aubergines (eggplant) in batches until browned on both sides. Add more oil, as necessary. Drain on kitchen paper (kitchen towels).

3 Put the beef, onion and garlic in a saucepan and cook over a medium heat, stirring, until browned. Add the tomato purée (paste), tomatoes, Worcestershire sauce, marjoram or oregano and salt and pepper. Simmer, stirring occasionally, for 10 minutes. Add the olives and (bell) pepper and cook for a further 10 minutes.

4 Bring a pan of salted water to the boil. Add the spaghetti and 1 tbsp olive oil and cook until tender, but still firm to the bite. Drain and turn the spaghetti into a bowl. Add the meat mixture and cheese and toss with 2 forks.

5 Arrange aubergine (eggplant) slices over the base and up the sides of the cake tin (pan). Add the spaghetti and then cover with the rest of the aubergine (eggplant) slices. Bake in a preheated oven at 200°C/400°F/ Gas 6 for 40 minutes. Leave to stand for 5 minutes, then invert on to a serving dish. Discard the baking parchment. Garnish with the fresh herbs and serve.

Beef & Pasta Bake

The combination of macaroni and beef korma gives this a really authentic flavour.

Serves 4

INGREDIENTS

900g/2 lb steak, cut into cubes
about 150 ml/¼ pint/⅝ cup
 beef stock
450g/1 lb dried macaroni
300 ml/½ pint/1¼ cups double
 (heavy) cream
½ tsp garam masala
salt
fresh coriander, to garnish

naan bread, to serve

KORMA PASTE:
6 garlic cloves
2.5 cm/1 inch piece fresh root ginger,
 coarsely chopped
60 g/2 oz/½ cup blanched almonds
6 tbsp beef stock
1 tsp ground cardamom

4 cloves, crushed
1 tsp cinnamon
2 large onions, chopped
1 tsp coriander seeds
2 tsp ground cumin seeds
pinch of cayenne pepper
6 tbsp of sunflower oil

1 To make the korma paste, grind the almonds finely using a pestle and mortar. Put the ground almonds and the rest of the korma paste ingredients into a food processor or blender and process to make a very smooth paste.

2 Put the steak in a shallow dish and spoon over the korma paste, turning to coat the steak well. Leave in the refrigerator to marinate for 6 hours.

3 Transfer the steak to a large saucepan, and simmer over a low heat, adding a little beef stock if required, for 35 minutes.

4 Meanwhile, bring a large saucepan of lightly salted water to the boil. Add the macaroni and cook for 10 minutes, until tender, but still firm to the bite. Drain the pasta thoroughly and transfer to a deep casserole. Add the steak, double (heavy) cream and garam masala.

5 Bake in a preheated oven at 200°C/400°F/Gas 6 for 30 minutes. Remove the casserole from the oven and allow to stand for about 10 minutes. Garnish the bake with fresh coriander and serve with naan bread.

VARIATION

You could also make this dish using diced chicken and chicken stock, instead of steak and beef stock.

Pasticcio

A recipe with both Italian and Greek origins, this dish
may be served hot or cold, cut into thick satisfying squares.

Serves 6

INGREDIENTS

250 g/8 oz/2 cups dried fusilli
1 tbsp olive oil, plus extra
    for brushing
4 tbsp double (heavy) cream
salt
fresh rosemary sprigs, to garnish
mixed salad, to serve

SAUCE:
2 tbsp olive oil
1 onion, thinly sliced

1 red (bell) pepper, cored, seeded
    and chopped
2 garlic cloves, chopped
600 g/1 lb 5 oz/5$\frac{1}{4}$ cups minced
    (ground) beef
400 g/14 oz can chopped tomatoes
125 ml/4 fl oz/$\frac{1}{2}$ cup dry white wine
2 tbsp chopped fresh parsley
60 g/2 oz can anchovies, drained and
    chopped
salt and pepper

TOPPING:
300 ml/$\frac{1}{2}$ pint/1$\frac{1}{4}$ cups natural
    yogurt
3 eggs
pinch of freshly grated nutmeg
40 g/1$\frac{1}{2}$ oz/$\frac{1}{2}$ cup freshly grated
    Parmesan cheese

1 To make the sauce, heat the oil in a frying pan (skillet) and fry the onion and red (bell) pepper for 3 minutes. Add the garlic and cook for 1 minute. Add the beef and cook until browned.

2 Add the tomatoes and wine to the pan and bring to the boil. Lower the heat and simmer for 20 minutes, until thickened.

Stir in the parsley and anchovies and season to taste.

3 Bring a pan of salted water to the boil. Add the pasta and oil and cook for 10 minutes, until almost tender. Drain and transfer to a bowl. Stir in the cream.

4 For the topping, beat the yogurt, eggs and nutmeg.

5 Brush an ovenproof dish with oil. Spoon in half the pasta and cover with half the meat sauce. Repeat, then spread over the topping and sprinkle with cheese.

6 Bake in a preheated oven at 190°C/375°F/Gas 5 for 25 minutes until golden. Garnish with rosemary and serve with a mixed salad.

Stuffed Cannelloni

Cannelloni, the thick, round pasta tubes, make perfect containers for close-textured sauces of all kinds.

Serves 4

INGREDIENTS

8 dried cannelloni tubes
1 tbsp olive oil
25 g/1 oz/^{1}/$_4$ cup freshly grated
   Parmesan cheese
fresh herb sprigs, to garnish

FILLING:
25 g/1 oz/2 tbsp butter

300 g/10^1/$_2$ oz frozen spinach,
   thawed and chopped
115 g/4 oz/^{1}/$_2$ cup ricotta cheese
25 g/1 oz/^{1}/$_4$ cup freshly grated
   Parmesan cheese
60 g/2 oz/^{1}/$_4$ cup chopped ham
pinch of freshly grated nutmeg
2 tbsp double (heavy) cream
2 eggs, lightly beaten

salt and pepper

SAUCE:
25 g/1 oz/2 tbsp butter
25 g/1 oz/^{1}/$_4$ cup plain
   (all purpose) flour
300 ml/^{1}/$_2$ pint/1^1/$_4$ cups milk
2 bay leaves
pinch of freshly grated nutmeg

1 To make the filling, melt the butter in a pan and stir-fry the spinach for 2–3 minutes. Remove from the heat and stir in the ricotta and Parmesan cheeses and the ham. Season with nutmeg, salt and pepper. Beat in the cream and eggs to make a thick paste.

2 Bring a pan of lightly salted water to the boil. Add the pasta and the oil and cook for 10–12 minutes, until almost tender. Drain and set aside to cool.

3 To make the sauce, melt the butter in a pan. Stir in the flour and cook, stirring, for 1 minute. Gradually stir in the milk. Add the bay leaves and simmer, stirring, for 5 minutes. Add the nutmeg, salt and pepper. Remove from the heat and discard the bay leaves.

4 Spoon the filling into a piping bag and fill the cannelloni.

5 Spoon a little sauce into the base of an ovenproof dish. Arrange the cannelloni in the dish in a single layer and pour over the remaining sauce. Sprinkle over the Parmesan cheese and bake in a preheated oven at 190°C/375°F/ Gas 5 for 40–45 minutes. Garnish with fresh herb sprigs and serve.

Tagliatelle with Pumpkin

This unusual dish comes from the Emilia Romagna region.
Why not serve it with Lambrusco, the local wine?

Serves 4

INGREDIENTS

500 g/1 lb 2 oz pumpkin or butternut
  squash, peeled and seeded
3 tbsp olive oil
1 onion, finely chopped
2 garlic cloves, crushed
4–6 tbsp chopped fresh parsley

pinch of freshly grated nutmeg
about 250 ml/9 fl oz/1$^{1}/_{4}$ cups
  chicken or vegetable stock
115 g/4 oz Parma ham (prosciutto)
250 g/9 oz dried tagliatelle

150 ml/$^{1}/_{4}$ pint/$^{5}/_{8}$ cup double
  (heavy) cream
salt and pepper
freshly grated Parmesan cheese,
  to serve

1 Cut the pumpkin or butternut squash in half and scoop out the seeds with a spoon. Cut the pumpkin or squash into 1 cm/½ inch dice.

2 Heat 2 tbsp of the olive oil in a large saucepan. Add the onion and garlic and fry over a low heat for about 3 minutes, until soft. Add half the parsley and fry for 1 minute.

3 Add the pumpkin or squash pieces and cook for 2–3 minutes. Season to taste with salt, pepper and nutmeg.

4 Add half the stock to the pan, bring to the boil, cover and simmer for about 10 minutes, or until the pumpkin or squash is tender. Add more stock if the pumpkin or squash is becoming dry and looks as if it might burn.

5 Add the Parma ham (prosciutto) to the pan and cook, stirring frequently, for a further 2 minutes.

6 Meanwhile, bring a large saucepan of lightly salted water to the boil. Add the tagliatelle and the remaining oil and cook for 12 minutes, until tender, but still firm to the bite. Drain the pasta and transfer to a warm serving dish.

7 Stir the cream into the pumpkin and ham mixture and heat through. Spoon over the pasta, sprinkle over the remaining parsley and serve. Hand the grated Parmesan separately.

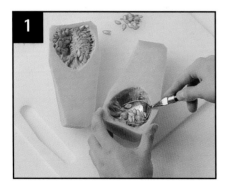

Tagliatelle with Chicken Sauce

Spinach ribbon noodles with a rich tomato sauce and topped with creamy chicken make a very appetizing dish.

Serves 4

INGREDIENTS

250 g/9 oz fresh green tagliatelle
1 tbsp olive oil
salt
fresh basil leaves, to garnish

TOMATO SAUCE:
2 tbsp olive oil
1 small onion, chopped

1 garlic clove, chopped
400 g/14 oz can chopped tomatoes
2 tbsp chopped fresh parsley
1 tsp dried oregano
2 bay leaves
2 tbsp tomato purée (paste)
1 tsp sugar
salt an pepper

CHICKEN SAUCE:
60 g/2 oz/4 tbsp unsalted butter
400 g/14 oz boned chicken breasts,
   skinned and cut into thin strips
90 g/3 oz/^{3}/4 cup blanched almonds
300 ml/^{1}/2 pint/1^1/4 cups double
   (heavy) cream
salt and pepper

1 To make the tomato sauce, heat the oil in a pan over a medium heat. Add the onion and fry until translucent. Add the garlic and fry for 1 minute. Stir in the garlic, tomatoes, parsley, oregano, bay leaves, tomato purée (paste), sugar and salt and pepper to taste, bring to the boil and simmer, uncovered, for 15–20 minutes, until reduced by half. Remove the pan from the heat and discard the bay leaves.

2 To make the chicken sauce, melt the butter in a frying pan (skillet) over a medium heat. Add the chicken and almonds and stir-fry for 5–6 minutes, until the chicken is cooked through.

3 Meanwhile, bring the cream to the boil in a small pan over a low heat and boil for about 10 minutes, until reduced by almost half. Pour the cream over the chicken and almonds, stir and

season to taste with salt and pepper. Set aside and keep warm.

4 Bring a large pan of lightly salted water to the boil. Add the tagliatelle and olive oil and cook until tender, but still firm to the bite. Drain and transfer to a warm serving dish. Spoon over the tomato sauce and arrange the chicken sauce down the centre. Garnish with the basil leaves and serve immediately.

Tortellini

Tortellini were said to have been created in the image of the goddess Venus's navel.
Whatever the story, these delicate filled pasta swirls offer a delicious blend of Italian flavours.

Serves 4

INGREDIENTS

115 g/4 oz boned chicken breast,
  skinned
60 g/2 oz Parma ham (prosciutto)
40 g/1¹/₂ oz cooked spinach,
  well drained
1 tbsp finely chopped onion
2 tbsp freshly grated
  Parmesan cheese

pinch of ground allspice
1 egg, beaten
450 g/1 lb Basic Pasta Dough (see
  page 4)
salt and pepper
2 tbsp chopped fresh parsley,
  to garnish

SAUCE:
300 ml/¹/₂ pint/1¹/₄ cups single
  (light) cream
2 garlic cloves, crushed
115 g/4 oz button mushrooms,
  thinly sliced
4 tbsp freshly grated Parmesan
  cheese

1 Bring a pan of seasoned water to the boil. Add the chicken and poach for about 10 minutes. Cool slightly, then put in a food processor, with the Parma ham (prosciutto), spinach and onion and process until finely chopped. Stir in the Parmesan cheese, allspice and egg and season to taste.

2 Thinly roll out the pasta dough and cut into 4–5 cm/ 1¹/₂–2 inch rounds.

3 Place ¹/₂ tsp of the filling in the centre of each round. Fold the pieces in half and press the edges to seal. Then wrap each piece around your index finger, cross over the ends and curl the rest of the dough backwards to make a navel shape. Re-roll the trimmings and repeat until all the dough is used up.

4 Bring a pan of salted water to the boil. Add the tortellini, in

batches, bring back to the boil and cook for 5 minutes. Drain and transfer to a serving dish.

5 To make the sauce, bring the cream and garlic to the boil in a small pan, then simmer for 3 minutes. Add the mushrooms and half the cheese, season and simmer for 2–3 minutes. Pour the sauce over the tortellini. Sprinkle over the remaining Parmesan cheese, garnish with the parsley and serve.

Spaghetti al Tonno

The classic Italian combination of pasta and tuna is enhanced in this recipe with a delicious parsley sauce.

Serves 4

INGREDIENTS

200 g/7 oz can tuna, drained
60 g/2 oz can anchovies, drained
250 ml/9 fl oz/1$\frac{1}{8}$ cups olive oil

60 g/2 oz/1 cup roughly chopped flat
leaf parsley
150 ml/$\frac{1}{4}$ pint/$\frac{5}{8}$ cup crème fraîche
450 g/1 lb dried spaghetti

25 g/1 oz/2 tbsp butter
salt and pepper
black olives, to garnish
crusty bread, to serve

1 Remove any bones from the tuna. Put the into a food processor or blender, together with the anchovies, 225 ml/ 8 fl oz/1 cup of the olive oil and the flat leaf parsley. Process until the sauce is smooth.

2 Spoon the crème fraîche into the food processor or blender and process again for a few seconds to blend thoroughly. Season to taste with salt and black pepper.

3 Bring a large pan of lightly salted water to the boil. Add the spaghetti and the remaining olive oil and cook until tender, but still firm to the bite.

4 Drain the spaghetti, return to the pan and place over a medium heat. Add the butter and toss well to coat. Spoon in the sauce and quickly toss into the spaghetti, using 2 forks.

5 Remove the pan from the heat and divide the spaghetti between 4 warm individual serving plates. Garnish with the olives and serve immediately with warm, crusty bread.

VARIATION

If liked, you could add 1–2 garlic cloves to the sauce, substitute 25 g/1 oz/½ cup chopped fresh basil for half the parsley and garnish with capers instead of black olives.

Spaghetti with Smoked Salmon

*Made in moments, this is a luxurious dish
to astonish and delight unexpected guests.*

Serves 4

INGREDIENTS

450 g/1 lb dried buckwheat spaghetti
2 tbsp olive oil
90 g/3 oz/$^{1}/_{2}$ cup crumbled
   feta cheese
salt
fresh coriander (cilantro) or parsley
   leaves, to garnish

SAUCE
300 ml/$^{1}/_{2}$ pint/1$^{1}/_{4}$ cups double
   (heavy) cream
150 ml/$^{1}/_{4}$ pint/$^{5}/_{8}$ cup whisky
   or brandy
125 g/4$^{1}/_{2}$ oz smoked salmon
pinch of cayenne pepper

black pepper
2 tbsp chopped fresh coriander
   (cilantro) or parsley

1 Bring a large pan of lightly salted water to the boil. Add the spaghetti and 1 tbsp of the olive oil and cook until tender, but still firm to the bite. Drain the spaghetti, return to the pan and sprinkle over the remaining olive oil. Cover, shake the pan, set aside and keep warm.

2 Pour the cream into a small saucepan and bring to simmering point, but do not let it boil. Pour the whisky or brandy into another small saucepan and bring to simmering point, but do not allow it to boil. Remove both pans from the heat and mix together the cream and whisky or brandy.

3 Cut the smoked salmon into thin strips and add to the cream mixture. Season to taste with cayenne and black pepper. Just before serving, stir in the chopped fresh coriander (cilantro) or parsley.

4 Transfer the spaghetti to a warm serving dish, pour over the sauce and toss thoroughly with 2 large forks. Scatter over the crumbled feta cheese, garnish with the coriander (cilantro) or parsley leaves and serve immediately.

COOK'S TIP

*Serve this rich and luxurious dish
with a green salad tossed in a
lemony dressing.*

Seafood Lasagne

This is one of those recipes where you can use any fish and any sauce you like: from smoked finnan haddock with a little whisky sauce to cod with cheese sauce.

Serves 4

INGREDIENTS

450 g/1 lb finnan haddock, filleted, skin removed and flesh flaked
115 g/ 4 oz prawns (shrimp)
115 g/4 oz sole fillet, skin removed and flesh sliced
juice of 1 lemon

60 g/2 oz/4 tbsp butter
3 leeks, very thinly sliced
60g/2 oz/^{1}/$_2$ cup plain (all purpose) flour
about 600 ml/1 pint/2^1/$_3$ cups milk
2 tbsp clear honey

200g/7 oz /1^3/$_4$ cups grated mozzarella cheese
450g/1 lb pre-cooked lasagne
60 g/2 oz/^{2}/$_3$ cup freshly grated Parmesan cheese
black pepper

1 Put the haddock fillet, prawns (shrimp) and sole fillet into a large bowl and season with black pepper and lemon juice. Set aside while you start to make the sauce.

2 Melt the butter in a large saucepan. Add the leeks and cook, stirring occasionally, for 8 minutes. Add the flour and cook, stirring constantly, for 1 minute. Gradually stir in enough milk to make a thick, creamy sauce.

3 Blend in the honey and mozzarella cheese and cook for a further 3 minutes. Remove the pan from the heat and mix in the fish and prawns (shrimp).

4 Make alternate layers of fish sauce and lasagne in an ovenproof dish, finishing with a layer of fish sauce on top. Generously sprinkle over the grated Parmesan cheese and bake in a preheated oven at 180°C/ 350°F/Gas 4 for 30 minutes. Serve immediately.

VARIATION

For a cider sauce, substitute 1 finely chopped shallot for the leeks, 300 ml/½ pint/1¼ cups cider and 300 ml/½ pint/1¼ cups double (heavy) cream for the milk and 1 tsp mustard for the honey.
For a Tuscan sauce, substitute 1 finely chopped fennel bulb for the leeks and omit the honey.

This is a Parragon Book
First published in 2003

Parragon
Queen Street House
4 Queen Street, Bath, BA1 1HE, UK

ISBN: 1-40540-829-4

Printed in China

NOTE

This book uses imperial and metric measurements. Follow the same
units of measurement throughout; do not mix imperial and metric. All
spoon measurements are level; teaspoons are assumed to be 5 ml and
tablespoons are assumed to be 15 ml. Unless otherwise stated, milk is
assumed to be whole milk, eggs and individual vegetables such as pota-
toes are medium, and pepper is freshly ground black pepper.

The times given for each recipe are an approximate guide only because
the preparation times may differ according to the techniques used by different people and the cooking times may vary as a result of the type of
oven used.

Recipes using raw or very lightly cooked eggs should be avoided by
infants, the elderly, pregnant women, convalescents and anyone suffer-
ing from an illness.